Mingle

Mingle

Caleb Parkin

Nine
Arches
Press

Mingle
Caleb Parkin

ISBN: 978-1-916760-06-6
eISBN: 978-1-916760-07-3

First published October 2024 by:

Nine Arches Press
Unit 14, Sir Frank Whittle Business Centre,
Great Central Way, Rugby.
CV21 3XH
United Kingdom

www.ninearchespress.com

Printed on recycled paper in the United Kingdom by Imprint Digital.

Nine Arches Press is supported using public funding by Arts Council England.

Supported using public funding by
ARTS COUNCIL
ENGLAND

For my friends (and my foes)

Contents

III.

"Pardon my asking, but do you think I could drink
this and be okay? I am still learning the scents

of poisons, can't yet smell them in the wild. Sip it
and tell me if you die."
                    – Kaveh Akbar, 'Aubade'

"I can't even find a pond small enough
to drown in without being ostentatious"
                    – Frank O'Hara, *Lunch Poems*

"It's one of the biggest hits of Britney Spears' career,
but fans are only just realising that the iconic opening
to *Toxic* is actually a sample."
                    – *Huffington Post*

Mingling Ritual
after C A Conrad

go into the kitchen
fling the cupboard doors asunder
grab at the packets of food   rip open
wok-ready noodles   oatcakes   a bucket of peanut butter

       (should anyone challenge you
           say that this process is the opposite
              of waste)

    sink your whole palm in
    the Nutella   or whatever   your poison   wear
    the packets of pasta   like crunchy mittens
    open tins of chickpeas   butterbeans
    delve your fingers into cans   like legumey
    earthworms   questing   whatever you have

          feel it on your fingertips   do not wash
          your hands   between foodstuffs   allow
          the aquafaba to moisten the dried
          fusilli   acknowledge the oats   in the teabags
          bear witness   to the contamination

      as you touch each raisin welcome every crinkly
      story at your fingertips   their life in earth
      their full moon harvesting   their desiccation
      feel yourself wither   in the vivacious sun
      then become processed   if you do not know

    what a nutmeg is   allow it to speak through
    the dark ridges   of its grated hemisphere
    now smear your hand   across an untouched week
    in your diary   when you reach that time
    you will register   the emanating odour

then think about   BICYCLES
their mechanisms & textures   their character & potential
if you have a bicycle   go & touch it all over
tickle under its mudguards   stroke its oily rims

      wipe these too across your diary   returning
      to today's pencilled appointments   next time you notice   a bicycle
      or whenever you travel   or think about travelling
      journey between   mechanisms &   food   in your mind

         eat every meal like a cycle
         up a severe gradient
         see each bicycle as a last meal
         keep in mind always the beginnings of things

I.

keep in mind always the beginnings of things

should you almost step on
the wrinkled pink nub of a bird
fallen   you suppose   having only just
twisted from its egg   soft beak groping

into sunlight   among silver birch branches
their pale buds quaking   ghastly with light-
hunger   so you look above to each
fork in that trunk   hunt evidence of nests

to plot the trajectory of this fall   as if
to know means anything   as if
to trace the cause is a cure

SEXTANK

giant isopod erotica

you better twerk-twitch your segments
over   haul that pale-lilac-plated-ass right
here   so we can grind those seven pairs

of *pereiopods*   my god imagine our
mancae babes   imagine each of their
identical names   say each of them

from each   of your four   sets of jaws
they'll be just like us   those microgiants
just add you   me   a sprinkle   of sulphur

just add my built-in Birkin *marsupium*
bursting with eggs and determination
light my fuse and don't   stand   back

we are sextanks   seabed bullets
feel these hydrothermal vents
crumble   crack   with our heat

Glossary:

Marsupium: "Mature females develop a brood pouch or marsupium when sexually active, the pouch being formed by overlapping oostegites or brood plates grown from the medial border of the pereiopods".

Pereiopods: each of the eight walking limbs of a crustacean such as a crab or lobster, growing from the thorax.

Mancae: young isopods emerge from the marsupium as miniatures of the adults, known as mancae.

Alfresco

yet cruising areas, littered with used condoms and cigarette butts, seem sacrosanct

– *National Post* (Vancouver), 2007

O boys   perhaps you needed
          a place to rest your knees
                    a clearing to feel soft breezes
          on those over-covered parts
                    of yourselves   maybe for smoke
                    to roil from your mouths
                              like c u m u l u s   clouds
                    which rumble in   threaten
          to break you up   with sharp
     prickles   unless   in high summer
          its arrival on backs   flanks
                    is felt   only after   in its flows
          across bodily contours   which sway
                    in time   to branches   whose tips   cymbal
                    under raindrops   those pines   conical   pinnacles
                              yawning   cathedral fingers   skyward

                                        *

O boys   in blue   your rumbling cars   sirens primed
if tissues   are the issue   install a bin
          and if butts   are the issue
          pop an ashtray down
and if the mattress   is the issue   isn't it better here   than landfill
and if the dogwalkers are the issue   have you seen what dogs
          get up to   right there   in the middle   of that manicured lawn

                                        *

yet not for me   on this green rock   of drizzle   cold
loathing   its constant tremble   of menace   in its country

side   too many options   exposed   in small hometowns
like mine   parks too small   hamsters   vying   for a single

wheel   sex outdoors   the preserve of warmer lands
braver men   though once   Mallorca   we were briefly

warm enough   alone enough   to shed ourselves amongst
lizards   and once   our soggy suburb   was arid   for weeks

until rain came   warm and languid   fat drops coming
each   with its own   aplomb   we turned off   security lights

stood in the garden   letting rain   trace our outlines
body-warm   our circulation   outside us   like trees

cocooned in vines   leaving the shape of two
men   pulsing   in the miracle   of mud

Whiptail Manifesto

each season the lizard switcheroo
though who is who in all-female
colonies is of course moot

in the rutting season run-up   they lie
stiffly one on another   like crusty baguettes
left out in bright   *obligate parthenogenesis*

their scales tessellate   are Teflon   from our ideas
this behaviour known as *pseudocopulation* with
a 'male-like role'   a 'female-like role'

what's with all the *likes* and un-likely likenesses
when these unisexualists have been doing this
since before *Homo sapiens sapiens* even got a grip

on walking on land   breathing air   she and her
are hybrid lovers   with hybrid lives   who hybridise
and need zero sperm   to turn out   their pearly clutch

Centaur

Based on instances of mounting, thrusting, and vocalisations,
the team concludes that these relations were, in fact, sexual.
– National Geographic website, 2019

Yee-haw! go the monkeys, *Ride 'em!*
swashbuckling on stags' backs:

> little showjumpers overcome by deer
> power, dreaming of future generations

of sika-macaque centaur. Or perhaps
their only spur is that instant

> of simian-on-quadruped fur?
> They cackle, pull antlers back,

shimmy and leap into leaves as another
stag feels a leapfrogging macaques' embrace

> on haunches, but continues grazing, alert
> for predators, film crews – voyeurs.

But who among us hasn't dreamed
of borrowing from another, becoming

> a strangest stranger, whose body
> is unmapped forest? Here they are,

these pioneers, who hypothesise,
combine hooves and prehensile tails

> to gallop under tomorrow's
> canopy, then above it too:

> whose gorgeous horns
> will disrupt the leaves.

The Landscape of Fear

You don't need a million wolves running around to restore an ecosystem.
– Liana Zanette, University of Western Ontario

Scurrying past the stadium, I ruminate,
startled by a lad-cub stomping his foot

> in my path. This cub, from a pack
> of lumberjack shirts who snort, pat

his lumberjack-shirted back. Little
protégé, unsettling his prey: setting

> down tracks, unsettling scent-trails,
> his howls bouncing off glass ravines.

At full-time, captive howls resound
loud enough to fracture pints, glasses.

> Lines drawn on these fractured paths:
> my thoughts scatter into dark cracks,

my silence spattered on their snouts.
Hurrying by the hospital, I ruminate.

Hornet

Hench horror, I'd love
to love you but
you've been at the 'roids
again, hyper-pumped, hitting
this city for punishable
flesh to pierce. You saw me
once, in the shower, loomed
thickly through steam,
your stabby appendage
strapped to that warning-
tape arse. So, I crushed you
in my swimmers, *crunch*
against the glass. The heft
of you! Your magnified parts!
You are the gruff one
in a zombie movie
who wants to toss
someone like me
out the fortified gates.
You're that boy who
lobbed a basketball
right at my face.
Let me in, you say,
thudding the cubicle –
See how magnificent I am,
pulsing thorax –
In my mass, my fury.

Infinity Mirror

On the dashboard of Elon's Tesla Roadster,
the one which was fired into space,
there's a smaller Tesla Roadster with its own replica
dummy driver, 'Starman', with one hand on the wheel,
elbow rested on the window. And presumably,
on the dashboard of that tiny Tesla, there's another,
tinier Tesla and an even tinier Starman, shrinking
like Matryoshka dolls – tech-bro in tech-
bro, a holographic generation. Over winter,

aphids can be born pregnant: embryos form
as they gestate. In this way, they survive the icy nothing
before spring: 30 to 40 generations until warmth arrives.
Then, the family grows again, gene pool expanding
into extended family. In each of the tinier Starmen,
their miniscule helmets – ellipsoid spawn, oily stars
poised to hatch into supernova, littering the night sky
with glinting glitter. Each tiny visor full of space,
Earth's reflection a dot within a dot inside a dot.

Hotel Hydrocarbon

the reviews don't mention the bioluminescent stink-
horns   their scorched stench   *does every room have these?*

YES the receptionist replies *THEY ARE NATIVE
TO THIS HOTEL* he wears a boiler suit hotel logo stitched

near the heart next to a hot-rock hole the pool shimmers iridescent
mists the flowerbed soil sighs white steam at dinner

the set main is polycyclic aromatic hydrocarbons
with <u>aromatic</u> underlined *what are hydrocarbons?*

AROMATIC IS WHAT THEY ARE SIR
as they slap a charred stack of gristle on my tray

*

at night coughing pierces the thin walls
puce wallpaper thick with paraffin Pall Malls

the hacking intensifies could be the boiler room's
echo i lock in for the night outside LEDs make

dark jokes about moonlight a cab passes every three
-to-five minutes its stereo glitches *with a taste of a poison paradise*

*

in the morning the polyester flower in the plastic vase
on the vinyl tablecloth has wilted the alluring smell of

chlorine you go poolside unclench a sun-lounger shroud it
in a mottled towel the water's brochure glitter in your eyes

as you rotate   on printed neon sprinkles   of a donut ring
GOOD MORNING   the pool-cleaner sifts aquamarine

algaecide   scoops up a shape   your face   his net wriggling
with this mask   he wears   as you pursue him   fumbling   foot-

prints evaporating   to beneath   where a heavy door clunks
his thick sigh locked   behind it   you shouldershove until a

yellowy backdraft creeps under   congeals around your feet

meditation   as king canute

the day I sat with the whole breath
of a tide   there was fog   bright sun
smudged behind   making vapour
warm and enveloping   I heeded

sand's songs as it prickled with
worm-bubbles   citizens at rest
sighing too   the tide was low
the moment between inhale ex-

hale empty   the moon held the water
stretched flat   like a robe   silken
and utterly clear   my courtiers
sea-urchins   rough-bristling

with dead man's fingers   bulbous
on rocks   their jewellery   limpets
and hermits   bargaining shack-shells
the fog persisted   the water released

from the moon's massy grip   anemone
tendrils   switch seaward   land-ho
water   stew-thick   antediluvian   rises
breath-warm   to my toes   to my ankle

thigh   and I am guzzled   by sea
clutching a mermaid's   empty purse
sunken to my crown   my story
garbled   in undercurrents

19 Gigabecquerels

Touch it, they warn, you'll get burns.
Cradle it for longer, who knows what
your cells will do – spill their borders,
pour themselves into new masses.
At 8mm X 6mm, a glowing Tic-Tac in
gamma-ray green, I presume. Shimmied, reports say,
through the hole where a bolt had shaken loose
in the outback, on its 1800km journey from mine
to deposit. Now, it radiates somewhere on a dirt track
or suburb, mocking Geiger counters. Caesium-137
hide 'n' seek. Perhaps between the fronds
of a roadside plant: seed of sickness, less needle in a haystack,
more breath-mint in an oil tanker. The streamlined size
of a suppository or pessary. *Erratum:*
An earlier version said the radiation source
was 19 becquerels, the correct figure
is 19 gigabecquerels. How abominable,
to be so tiny but contain so much.

Mrs Howorth's Irradiated Nuts

They are out there: on the Kentish coast,
or by unplumbed lochs in the Trossachs.
Muriel dashes the waxy packets to the Post Office,
thinks, *Even the wheel was novel once* – as postie's bike
whirls past the TV shop, where bright cathode-ray tubes
annihilate geography. She affixes each stamp; bright tongue
flicking, a hummingbird-moth.

                  A reporter is *en route* to photo-
graph her irradiated peanut plant. How it germinated
with gusto, grew with such modern vim. *The first
of its kind*, she'll inform him, *and the only. Imagine*,
she'll fizz, *what else we might uncover when we
crack open the seeds of the atom, let its bounty
glow upon us.*

            In the United States now, Soviets too, and especially
in blasted Japan, those wedge-shaped beds
of discovery. *Nature*, (and here, she will widen
her eyes) *proceeds by theme and variation, so why not
up the tempo?* Muriel slurps grapefruit, stabs each
segment – wan, lacking – then spits pips. *Room*,
she incises, *for improvement*.

              Unlocking her door, she pictures
the Gamma Gardens' high walls; the Cobalt-60 bunkers
at their epicentres. Shrivelled specimens up front;
eruptions of promise, further back. The Source
concealed in its isotopic sarcophagus – what wonders
might those white coats discover: Edenic stalks?
Roots, no wind or rain can outwit?

              She skips to her peanut progeny,
verdant with her name; pictures her 573 Mutation Experimenters
greeting Mr Speas' *energised seeds* – forms blank and hungry
for data. No matter the improbability of utility.

                 The questing is the thing.

She pricks her lapel with concentric jade. Her earth-brown poly-
skirt distended with petticoat. In the atom, she will say,
she has found – a home? No. A masquerade, replete
with exotic strangers: a waltz, a gavotte, a vortex –

     she totters, composes, dots each wrist with peppermint,
pirouettes again to the chimes of her ingenuity. The door
ajar, its ring peals

              and Muriel a nucleus, about to split –

Ricinus in Spring, 2020

a golden shovel after Sylvia Plath, 'Poppies in July'

Hot, silent April. You sit at a little
Formica table, enquire about this bloody
egg cup, full of reddish water. He skirts
the issue, says it's just a seed, resting there
to soak, preparing for the ground. *There are*
poisons everywhere, he whispers. *Fumes*
in airducts which life has colonised, nature that
flourishes in death. He sips oolong, goes on, *I*
will plant it at the edge of the bed, but you cannot
mistake it for food, cannot smoke it or touch
its spiky leaves. Now you can't recall where
Ricinus has rooted, in which spot its toxins are
concealed. His grubby palms gesture to your
garden. And you imagine all the opiates
erupting from Afghan fields, the pollens in your
nostrils, the masses in cities' tubes. Nauseous,
you open a cupboard, swollen with capsules.

II.

Self-Portrait as Diary

my skin is matt black nylon
my guts   boxy pages in
week-to-view   with spaces

for different lists
endocrine: pineal adrenal testicle
nervous: ganglia radial spinal

today i check inside   myself
for availability   then take
myself out   for breakfast

i eat time   speak in days
try to order a latte but
it comes out as *October*

i flap a section of innards
at the bewildered barista
try to order food by flicking

through June - September
then cough and numbers
spray out: *30   31   28   29*

my chatter is scrawled lists
marked with arrows> asterisks*
my thought track neatly lined

in a corner by the door   i file
myself   the breeze picks random
weeks   to dream in   the future's

pristine pages   my unfilled months
their whiteness   like a sky   you think
is going to snow   but never will

Our South African National Parks

103 pages, 25cm X 20cm, English/Afrikaans

Ek is *Ons Suid Afrkaanse Nasionale Wildtuine*
and my cover is open. Startled antelope gather   (cornered)

in faded sepia near a handwritten note: *To Joy /*
With Love from / Aunt Cecily. I am replete

with cards from *United Tobacco Co's. (South) Ltd:*
A BULL ELEPHANT, impressive close-up. Chapter One:

The Importance of Wildlife Sanctuaries. Page seven, a map   (so jolly)
Johannesburg's mining tower; Cape Town's grapes;   (so potent, so copious)

in Mozambique, a nameless local, yoked with fruit.   (faceless, posed)
My spine worn away, revealing glued clusters of pages.   (covers unhinged
                                like a barged-in door)

*

Once, I was fresh-printed
and brilliant in Cecily's lap

                              (Great-Great Aunt)

sat amongst stacks of spent packets

                                (the acrid tar
                                of stacked leaves
                                each a rolled note)

NO. 10 VULTURES FEEDING
        AASVOËLS VREET

                            (I should light you up
                            a monolithic cigar

NO. 26   GEVLEKTE WOLF
        SPOTTED HYENA

                        let your matter be known
                        cindered in my lungs)

The Game Protection Society of the Transvaal
Wild Life Protection Society of South Africa

(cordoned-off   in a continent
scarred by imperious geometry)

*

EVENING SCENE ON A RIVER BANK
Kruger National Park

(the monochrome of zebras
lined and powerful   like books
they merge in heat haze collective
camouflage   puzzling predators)

Wild animals are very foolish
in respect to motor traffic

(how Great Aunt Nancy visited   gifted
a single ostrich feather   and I chose
to see it   wafted   into her train window)

the destruction of habitats
is   no doubt   the manifestation
of some deep-seated instinct in Man
inherited from his primitive ancestors

(how Granny Joy othered
her *brethren*   and I chose
only to hear   her fraternity)

between the Sabi and Olifants rivers...
burgers of the Republic for services rendered...
a free hunting ground whenever they so desired...

(how this book heavied my shelf
but I only allowed myself to read
its   collectable   menagerie)

35

BERGZEBRA NASIONALE RESERVATE

(a band of cartoon zebras   on this map
reams and reams of their originals
once galloped   savannahs   their
library of thunder   expired   an echo)

*

Details from my depiction of the Indian Ocean:
    figure on a fishing dinghy held
    aloft on a whale's blowhole   (so jolly)

    another whale   (impaled)
    by a steam ship   (harpooned)
    puff-puffing   (merrily merrily
                                                      like cigarillo smoke)

    a keepnet slung out   (a banner
    by Cape Town   an imposition)

    where fish shoal gleefully in   (grinning)

    a mermaid and merman   (Caucasian)
    sat on a rock   she regards herself in a mirror   (or offers a tray
                                                        of roe   for Him)

    by Durban a spiky-backed fish
    with an amusingly long nose   (Pinocchio Pinocchio)

    by East London Neptune   Poseidon   (imported gods)
    Masters of the ocean   (his sneery-leer)
    watch over fishermen   (drunk in charge
                                                       of His trident again)

a figure dives   scuttles his skiff   (my aunt posts photos
                                                    of my Great Great Grandfather
                                                    with his powerful moustache

something like a seahorse   when I mention
held on the sea's rough surf   this says not to mention
                                                        the family name)

two penguins   (marooned
on a tiny island   on sharp rocks)
by Port Elizabeth

impeccable calligraphic waves   (oceans   on paper
                                                        the whiteness

                between every ship)

                        *

I am less a book

                                                    (more a mirror)

see your reflection stretch

                                                    (*impressive close-up*)

                in the pools settling in my serifs
                    (my thick   ivory   skin)

                    I am your history
                    (smoking gun   of   kin)

Presence

as you loom overhead
stare down at the swirl
of scalps arranged around
the table's disc   you'll say
I   am   not   the   room

but they will not hear
because your voice is light
precise from every flicker
of chandelier   you'll say
I am not the room repeat it

like wallpaper   the phrase
growing thorns to barb
the fractured ceiling rose
you'll say it muffled from
beneath the well-worn rug

hard as oak floorboards
you'll say it solidly as each chair
knocked back   prostrate
flaring out from the table
you'll shout it   warped as

lead-lined windowpanes
I   am   not   the   room
portcullis on your upper lip
but still   their cycle circles
clock trappings   fixtures

vibrate with your voice
as you feel all the spiders
hunker into cracks in your
plaster   their jaws in unison
mutter something about

this room   its closetful
of furs   each iron hanger
rattles   skeleton of mink
bone rabbitbone wolfbone
hollow syncopation of joints

cracked-skull windchimes
dissonant murmur of ribs

AUCTION

(Tetrachloroethlyene)

                                        a successful dry cleaner
                                                        continuation of

                        extensive
        machine
                    remainder

    The property
                        internally
                            double

                            with

                    wonderful

                                            previously

                                                    un   stated

                    details.

Erasure poem from online property auction listing.

Nature Is (Not) Healing

a meme ekphrastic

It lifts Tower Bridge's gates,
sends through its envoy: a 100
-foot tall yellow rubber duck.

It refills the rivers with Crocs:
their holey rubbery skins
and strappy-backed grins.

And Nature sees this is good:
sends brontosauruses to graze
at Times Square's empty screens.

The Hudson is naturally day-glo
again, replete with shell-suited dolphins,
collies on surfboards; waving penguins.

From the Tyne, the long necks
of inflatable penises peek out
after cowering under grimy tides.

In Bury, all colours of creature –
Tinky-Winky purple, to reddest
Po – scamper the echoing station.

There are cows on the roofs, where
they belong. Godzilla cheers over
Piazza San Marco. Manatees spray

the White House fountains. And from
immaculate Dubai streets, the Burj
Khalifa tickles a sky so cloudless

we can see the entire solar system
bumping together like a commuter
train, a little emptier than before.

Mickey Pandemic

C_6H_6

never accept sanitiser from a dude
with white gloves surgically attached

what is in that bottle he carries   branded
with his face   tiny   benzene-laced

turn it around   there's a white skull
with great round ears over two crossed murine bones

he motions   you hold out cupped hands
the gel fizzes   onto the forest of your skin

and when Mickey says *Sanitise* he means *Eradicate*
when he says *Destroys all bacteria*   he means business

Serving Dragon's Blood on the Escape Pod

Mercury sulfide (HgS)

Don't let the birds fool you, the delicate foliage:
this dish is pure volcano. Its glaze, luscious

sulphur. Heat it up. Mercury from Earth's sticky
core will claw your nerves, enticing you to quake.

Go on: fondle this cracked ceramic. Each vol-au-vent
is a thermal vent, a nostril's smoulder. Every canapé

means inferno, petrifying the bright forests of your inscape.
This dish is a slice of plasma pudding, exquisitely carved

denouement. Eat. Learn what it is to taste a dragon's
sanguine mind, to sip its crystalline thoughts.

M, as a river

when you tap out missives
                on the tablet   sometimes whole
                        minutes pass by   you write in
                full paragraphs   formal   as though
        sending letters   from another
    neurological   time   zone
& I try not to look   as you type
        to wait   until you click
                the speaker icon   that stand-in for
                        your voice   when it becomes   dammed
                clogged   in a dopamine flow   & often
        the conversation   has moved on
        canalised   in its   industrial lines
        but in the pauses   falters
                of this dis-
                        ease you remain   paused
                    in the shadows of your
                synapses   rerouting   flowing around
        what   you want   to say   a shingle
        of layers   re-layering   in each
                of these   riverbends   these
        still spots   their flow   slowed   by in-
                directness
                        we can choose
                to rest   here   too   in these *U*s
                        amongst   searching roots
                    & burrows   we can try to wait

                in this meander   of talk   its unhurried current
                curving back on itself   a river's natural
                        state   following gravity   with pockets

                        full of s e d i m e n t   full   of   life

The Orca BnB

Each hour floodlights double through the nets' mesh. The heat turns from snowflake to five; the ceiling props slice, too low. The shutters open halfway, their corners jutting like rudders. I used to feel at home here. Now, speech masses plasticky in my sinuses – language popping in my teeth. My tongue is too large, body too long for these plundered beds, synthetic sheets. In the floor, pipes whoosh and click; the room's corners jagged as a superyacht. We used to feel at home here. You stir, and your snore thickens into Sonar – regimented beeps clotting in our airways. We float a pillow's shadow over your face, teach ourselves to breathe again.

Waterlily House

Victoria boliviana, Kew Gardens

By the door, three-foot leaves capsized:
their vascular undersides, umbilical stalks;
through wrought iron spirals enter
in this thick air, where lily pads hover
on a pool, circled in white concrete.
They surface, unfurl, spread pinkly –
spiny fogs that roil across the pond's
black membrane. The glass smirched with
plant-breath; climbers viscerate
from white iron Os on the rafters.
We circumambulate this cell:
how polished, staged, the way all bodies
are becoming. From within, you cannot see
those leaves, their palms pressed out
on greening panes, how
they long to permeate the skin.

We long to permeate this skin,
its greening panes. How
our leaves, their palms, press up,
are becoming from within. You cannot see
how polished, staged; the way our bodies
are circumambulated. This cell,
from the white iron Os of these rafters:
plant-breath. Climbers viscerate
black membranes on glass smirched with
spiny fogs that roil across our pond.
We surface, unfurl, spread pinkly
on our pool, circled in white concrete
in this thick air. We're lily pads, hovering
through wrought iron spirals. Enter
our vascular undersides, umbilical stalks,
these doors – three-foot leaves, capsized.

A pond in Maui turned pink

and it isn't toxic algae but nor should we swim, eat the fish. A photo opp – but should we be smiling? Single cells, drunk on seawater-salinity, doubled. It's an *Archaea* party! It's, like, something from the *Barbie* movie: their cute choreography, her journey on a pastel rocket to rollerblade in a neon-pink *fanny pack* on the California seafront. A flushed capillary, viewed from drone shots. The sea, cut off at a footbridge. How the *real world isn't what I thought it was*. A magenta scrap of water in three jagged prongs. The 1990s pink shell suit I loved – until I learned love was only permitted in certain *milieus*. Entire multiplexes pink, doors spilling like ruptured vessels. Scientists investigating this boy like something from *Barbie*. Some abundances are signs of environmental stress. *Halobacteria*: so motile and lurid and salty. Snug in pinkness, florid in drought. Like they'll overspill into this neon globe, UV-marbled in too-much sun. That shell suit, so pink it could tip the Pacific.

Queertopia (Working Title)

i dreamed it once   although
   some dream features never
      get shared publicly   this was
culty   based on *Rajneeshpuram*
         that fleeting Oregon city
         with its ecstatic polycules   clad
  from exclusively enlightened red-
    orange boutiques   but we all know
    how that ended
                ideals toxified with
Salmonella in water mains   on polling day
     a guru uncovered   skulking away
        in one of six gleaming Rollers

       *

i am putting off telling you
how we wore stylish tunics
     seemed always to be embracing
       in top-notch lighting   Clarendon filtered
the way some words from cardboard placards
had leapt off   each started their own parades
       perhaps it was sponsored by *Coke*
       but i was having one with each of you

maybe i am misremembering the goats'
tiny hoofs massaging our temples at yoga
       or the gym where we witnessed sprints
       of level-ten treadmill   in six-inch heels
how all the walls were cascades of devil's
ivy   which can thrive even in caves
       or the way we affirmed each
       and every other's *NO*

in my dream we orbited Earth
hands held so tight they sweated
       until the dream-lens welled up
       like a porthole on a sinking ship
and wouldn't it be perfect
if i had woken up crying

        *

i am still cruising the outskirts
of my dream   pointing outwards

to no-place   where the horizon
is still unblemished   beyond

the reality of being together   in this larger
together   which only wants us together

for our purchasing power   saying   *look
out there   just past where we can actually see*

GOLD

My fantasies and my very fertile imagination lead me [...] to the Baroque.
– Yves Saint Laurent

How it goes with everything.
How I can possess it, even though I cannot afford it.
How it used to underpin economies.
How Fort Knox will protect it,
      long after the soils have sighed their final crops.
How *Acanthus mollis* gilds its leaves in the sun;
how we relocated 'Hollard's Gold' and it wilted,
      then cascaded back from both beds.
How only the karat-initiated can detect authenticity.
How the world is awash with gorgeous fakery.
How I have a matching notebook and pen
      and trainers, in various shades of phoney.
How we adore it and perish in its name;
      its colour, its brilliance, its divine heaviness.
How in those bunkers, behind retinal scans
      and foot-thick steel, nobody will enjoy it
      interred beneath the deluges.
How on buttons, it is the jewellery of daytime.
How it stoppers *eau de parfums.*
How each sequin shimmers, eventually, into the sea.
How its variations are symphonic.
How it draws attention to itself.
How we mine for it still: mine; mine; mine.
How it pierces under stage lights, explodes from disco balls.
How it is surprisingly soft: lamé, brocade, leather.
How it is protected by razor-wire.
How it is the measure and the rule.
How it was a gift of wise men.
How nobody can ever be as good as it.
How once, we saw a watch in a jeweller's window
      worth more than our home.

How actors in films bite at coins.
How prospectors sifted the grains of themselves.
How Scrooge McDuck dove gleefully into it.
How it lies always beneath us.
How golden our hope is, approximately
        seven inches long, three-and-a-half inches wide,
        one and three-quarter inches thick.

I Found It Beautiful

for Paul Dirac

If this poem was about you, it might
have strayed into the florid and metaphorical.
It could, perhaps, have taken issue with your
assertion that science and poetry are incompatible:
the former, making difficult things understandable;
the latter, making simple things incomprehensible.

If this poem was about you, it might have invoked
the Scale of Strangeness at subatomic and human levels:
how your colleagues at Cambridge invented a *dirac*,
a unit equating to one word per hour; how you'd stare
at the ceiling for five minutes, the window five more,
then reply *Yes* or *No* – and were always, always right.

If this poem was about you, it may have riffed on
the universe as multiples of a charge of the electron;
the way two times three is not the same as three times two;
on vanishing gradients; how sons can become divisible
from fathers. How, when asked how you found
your equation, you said you *found it beautiful*.

But I want to try to speak plainly, and to you. To be
literal more than literary. I won't call you *Sir*
and respect that refusal. Take your time
replying: here is a clear window, a plain ceiling.
I will welcome your *Yes* or your *No*, try to trust you.

I'd like to know how to see beneath the surface
of matter, paint it with numbers – can you teach me?

I'd like to understand the way you wrote by thinking
the whole thing first, no editing – can you show me?

I'd like to see what it's like to take away all
these *likes,* to see life only as *is* – can you tell me?

I know you'll likely decline. Just as on that
cruise-liner with Heisenberg, you puzzled at why
he might dance. This is not an invitation to dance.
Nor a celebration: you always fled from those.
Not that it matters, but in this city

where you grew up, few know your name.
Unlike Schrödinger's hypothetical pet,
yowling and clumsy in off-the-cuff
chat. You are: one street sign; a sculpture
without text. You are held in matter, precise.

How to Be 2-D

get good at side-
stepping you'll
need to choose
a plane and stick
to it it's either x
or y but definite-
ly not both paper
is best trust in its
thinness its bare-
ly perceptible de-
pth even a tablet
screen risks persp-
ective or subst-
ance get used to
sidling walls sc-
uttling cock-
roachily ima-
gine your ab-
domen is a ba-
lloon at the v
end of a party
your body a f-
ormless sack
of former
breath all
of you
a flat-
pack
sch-
em-
atic

III.

Nuclear Beetroot

A conical room, carpeted scarlet-red: a velvety epithelium.
The whole structure, a dunce's cap. Table, low and tiny, redly

three-legged; wooden bucket of borscht; a litre of V8
juice to chase. Glug them both down and then wait.

The leaflets say to bear in mind *everything you bring*
today will be incinerated, except yourself, you guess.

You have brought a 1990s Gameboy, *Tetris*
its only option. Beetroot floods your trachea,

Red-Seas your stomach as you stack blocks,
slot them briskly into crowded screens

reflecting red like blocky viscera.
Every three minutes, a red laser

peels your body into data. Gut's
pink anaconda; nerves, a strontium

sparkler; skull rose-tinted, as you focus
on the tiny screen; piss flowing ever

more glowstick. Theme tune
cycling, cycling. That night,

you imagine the word
N i n t e n d o bubbling up

a chimney. Your eyelids
display cells, glitching

upwards, each one
refusing to tesselate.

What does cancer smell like to an ant?

Piss, initially. In that perfect round
petri dish. Like the old joke goes:

My ant has no nose. Except the reply is:
Incredibly. Each antenna, a telescopic nostril,

.

an olfactory multi-tool of receptors.
And perhaps that question, how one ant

smells, is – for a superorganism – moot.
They gather the periphery of this cesspool

from a test subject: flat golden pond of murine
urine. From above, they bristle its edges

like spikes from a naval mine or cloves
in a shrivelled Christingle. At this stage,

only ten minutes in, they have learned to linger
by tumorous piss a little longer, seeking a syrupy

reward. Collective sommelier, with a penchant
for *volatile organic compounds,* their feelers brush

the skin of the water like a lover or
pharmacist. They fuss its surface tension,

weaving with air. Are buffalo, encircling
crocodile-infected waterhole. Moving closer

– the microscopy of their eyes, the fine machinery
of their jaws – they do not recognise themselves.

Just as any of us might not, as we stand staring
into a bathroom's round mirror, one normal

Wednesday in winter, hearing the last ringtone
from an unknown number: a message left to

please, at your earliest convenience, call back, call back –

learning to spell 'leukaemia'

every time that surprise
'u' and intrusive 'a'
something to do with blood

that -*ia* suffix says *medicine*
when it pricks your speech
and you will question why

and for whom you are
divulging at all   when it drips
through layers of resistance

or incredulity and down
synapses to jabbing fingers
you wonder each time

why blood goes rogue
when bones go wrong
how body doesn't know

when to finish a cell's story
and so we give it its own
container   this canker

that word staring back
like a newsreader faltering
as the autocue whirls

It's not the years, honey, it's the mileage

Indiana Jones, *Raiders of the Lost Ark*

For each month of autumn, I add a supplement:
Omega-3, 5-HTP. As winter blots the windows,
the trees bare capillaries on lightbox skies – evermore

ostentatious adaptogens: Rhodiola, Ginseng, Holy Basil.
Within them is a different me, a capsule version who rises
before daylight into running shoes. Who is primed

for a schedule where each minute is a precious spore
to ingest. When I forget to take them, carefully stacked
in daily click-cases, I assume I will disintegrate,

like the mercenary in *Indiana Jones* who drank from
the wrong Grail. *He chose…poorly,* the ancient knight intones,
the Nazi's skin slipping from bone, hair strawing, skull

pestled into supernatural breezes. What will happen
without these precious additions? Each supplement
minecarts down the trackway of my gullet. I crave a map's

printed clarity; a comforting rendering of my innards;
my chaotic systems, illustrated. I can feel all my routes
towards addiction; the rich menu for my neurons

to dissolve. Something must arrive, neat in its pouch
through the door, through my mouth. Precise
in its dose of promise: a purer world, a future

in which my bronchioles' buds are
always springing forth, sticky green.

Two Tablespoonfuls

she asks the Crem for. Or maybe she asks for *two tablespoons*. The former, an official measure, the latter just a tag or moniker: *table-spoon, tablespoonful, Nanna, Mama*. Table-spoons part of the profusion of 18th-century spoons: *mustard-spoon, salt-spoon, half-spoon, step-spoon*.

She didn't ask for the equivalent 29.6 millilitres. How do you measure that from the cremulator? Can you enquire if it's more demerara or caster? Two tablespoons before the mass was interred; a sprinkle of grey icing on an earthy gateau. But if you pot a rose up on top, watch it wither.

Not dessertspoons, soupspoons. Both lack gravity. No, she required the best spoon / best-spoon / bestspoon. The Sunday roast spoon: anaemic slice of meat; peas unpodded; carrots, mushy suns. The favourite spoon.

Not three teaspoonfuls, those ten-a-penny, for-the-many everyday stirrers into anemic tea. *Two tablespoons* – for serving, eating. Not half a fluid ounce, because this was not fluid, more flour. Self-raising.

Was she forging a diamond? A pendant, to mount on a sceptre? Or would she funnel it to nestle in the spice rack between *Marjoram* and *Nutmeg?*

Way back, you carried a personal spoon to every table. No rows and rows of stainless-steel communal spoons, taking and sloughing off hyphens: *soupspoon, sugar-spoon. Love spoon*.

Two tablespoons. The table and the spoon, fused for an age by a hyphen, until they became a measure, a single unit. Those two loaded spoons she took, then fired that hyphen – a missile into the sun.

Burying the Sky

I.

in Diclofenac   this coda   this finale
clean fold   into economic flesh   ailing livestock
defer death   ideal   once laced   into landscapes
a slow cyanide   final denial   acidic fields
coiled ground   a clan of bills   ecocidal coins
docile   green bills   folded   enact   no fines
no felons   clean   economical   acid-laden
fold into   colic flesh   cancel this   land

II.

in Doongerwadi dhakma   add the bodies   ignore
the sky   drained of vulture adornment   hooked
beaks   ordained   to drain   the dead   iron of erosion
vultures   who wooed flesh   from odorous bone
who gnawed at the graw   of the devoted   a dodo
undoing   who grew ragged   with gut stones
did not know   the danger   of cattle   could not be
warned   vultures   renowned   for returning   flesh
to sky   who dined   on the wind of us   now die
with a roar   in their organs   dragged bodies toward
the bony core   rewind now   to a dawn   a dawning
wonder   realisation   of a sky raining   wings
a dawn   red with ending

Diclofenac is an anti-inflammatory drug given to cattle and which has been attributed to the decline of vulture numbers by more than 95% since the 1990s. **Doongerwadi dhakma** ('tower of silence') is a sky burial site in Mumbai, where bodies are, or were, left to be consumed by vultures.

Tomorrow's Yield

The sun begins to rise, dips again,
glitches above the slick horizon
seeking clouds to shelter behind.

My crop is reaching its peak, by which
I mean its most translucent, after weeks
of shoot and un-shoot, stuttering

half-growth, it erupts from crumbling
dark, locked on to a sun whose arc
is always a step traced, retraced.

Crows tread carefully – stand like code
on branches, look over stalk rows which
might any day start, cease, yield.

This field on a mezzanine of earth;
the ground would echo if you
stomped. The rain stutters in,

with a first reconnoitring burst, before
a shower commits, leaves a crisp stripe
of glittered columns: orderly water

en route to roots. If there is
a farmer, s/he/it is beyond my field
of vision – perhaps they stand

at the electrified edges of this space
and consider the value or value-
lessness of this crop.

Perhaps they chew on a bendy straw,
wear wellies pristine white, grasp
a programmable pitchfork.

Do they watch me now
as I watch the crescent moon
lift open, closed, open – months

blinked out like an eye ejecting dust?

Archive

Imagine a future in which these animals exist only as virtual-reality
holograms recreated from old television documentaries.
– Callum Roberts, in 'Shifting Baselines', *Granta: Second Nature* (2020)

the reality is not virtual but internal
and   having digitised those tens
of thousands of hours of footage

of whales breaching heroically
out of seascapes
colour-graded impeccable blue

macaws with their bright carnivals
of plumage outspread   impossible
squadrons   tree to endless off-camera tree

troupes of macaques in close-up
sifting each pixel of one another's
fur   divining for fleas

now all of these images are mapped
inwardly   a new nerve   fibre-optic
rooted to our vertebrae

when we feel joy   an overcoming
there's the humpback   its blowhole
rainbowing in the pure light

when we make love   bonobos
populate our bodies   puppeting
their acts in bedrooms   afforested

with tomorrow's shame

which we feel in us as the rising throb
of a hornet's nest   whose queen pulses at
our solar plexus   our extremities drone

each of our inscapes   unique
we cannot see what life scurries
or glides or stomps through another

there is no channel to the inside of us
only memories of a tune we each recall
try to hum to one another   off-
key   whole verses   forgotten

Narcissus Aesthetics: *Reflecting Perfection*™

bacterium Clostridium botulinum (Botox)

Thank you so much for choosing us, for choosing me
above all those other clinics: such choice now. Such choice!
Now, we do recognise you could have made this investment
with any of the other brands of borehole or wishing well, to gaze
down, seek your preferred reflection. You've met
the receptionist, yes – ignore her, ignore her. She is
a little too haunted by our clinical ethics.
You're safe with me and – yes – the resemblance is – well –
not quite what it could be – your you and my me:
just wait until we're through: today, then tomorrow,
next season, next decade. My needles galore are
a pine forest – bristling with pinpricks of tamed *botulinum*.
We'll smooth out those tidelines of time on your forehead, make you
a shiny new me. We'll claw out those crow's feet and fill your furrows,
your skin is as silken as mists lapping this forest floor.
Yes, thank you for coming all the way out here to find us.
We're so glad to be of service. We know – yes, we know
you'll be nervous this first time. The kiss of steel on your
epidermis. Hold still. Hold your breath. Hold this test tube,
this sharps bag, this cotton wool pad. That isn't a chorus, it's
the dawn. Stay with me. You're a valued partner.
Trust us. There is nobody here, only your me and mine.
Feel free to call the receptionist tomorrow, to tell
yourself how you are feeling. See if she is at her desk,
if you hear her warnings, just seek
this window in the ground. Dive towards me,
pierce our immaculate skin: I will always be here.

I will always be here, piercing our immaculate skin,
this window in the ground. Dive towards me
if you hear her warnings. Just seek
yourself, how *you* are feeling. See if she is at her desk
and feel free not to call the receptionist, tomorrow. Tell us,
trust us – there is nobody here, only your me and my
dawn chorus. Stay with me, your valued partner.
This sharps bag, this cotton wool pad, that isn't a chorus, it's
epidermis – hold still, hold my breath. Hold this test tube –
you'll be nervous this first time, the kiss of steel on your
us. Are we glad to be of service! We know. Yes, we know,
yes, thank you for coming all the way out here to find us,
your skin as silken as mists lapping this forest floor.
A shiny new me! We'll claw out those crow's feet and fill your furrows,
we'll smooth out those tidelines of time on your forehead, make you
a pine forest – bristling with pinpricks of tamed *botulinum.*
Next season, next decade, my needles galore are
just waiting until we're through. Today, then tomorrow:
not *quite* what it could be. Your you and my me,
you're safe with me and – yes – the resemblance is – well –
a little too haunted. Buy our clinical ethics
from reception desk. (Ignore her, ignore her. She is
down.) Seek *your* preferred reflection. You've met
many other brands of borehole or wishing well to gaze
anew, so we recognise you have made this investment
above all those other clinics. Such choice now, such choice –
so thank you so much for choosing us, for choosing me.

Ten Reflections on the Same Pond

1. Black-grey, rare earth, unrenewable
2. 30 – 40 per cent of the villagers
3. *Development first, clean-up later*
4. No reflections of the new high-rises
5. Teeth so brittle cattle cannot eat
6. *Outsourced danger.* Slow violence.
7. Leaching towards the 'mother river'
8. Green energy bubbles urgently
9. An old man holds his smartphone
10. his face reflected in its black-grey mirror.

O Saint Astronaut

your miracle was eating a candle
that night   out in the caravan
to detox   & if the moon is
cheese perhaps its beams glow
cheddar-yellow   & one lands
on the fold-down table   then in
your pale delirium   you reach
to moonlight   for sustenance
a waxy feast   the wick catching
at your throat as you gorge

perhaps then you wanted more
of course   did you want all
the moon had   every lumen
of curdled light   I wish I didn't
know what heroin smells like
but it became   your smell
the fumes through that dinky
caravan chimney   that candle
was the moon's envoy   come
to save you   Saint Moon pin-

pointing our suburban driveway
his anguished face   spitting rays
starbursts of candles landing by the
afflicted   saying   *consume my light*
let me waxen your innards   until nothing
no tinfoil no fumes no spirits will stick   nothing
will be so dark that this frictionless
moonlight cannot overcome it
this celestial meal   eat the candle

eat the whole   fucking   moon
be nourished with protons   even on
the damp floor of a squat   moonlight
will sate you   make itself manifest
on Earth   so praise be   Saint Moon
& God of Cheese   praise be Saint
Astronaut   you found ground again
stepped down from that caravan
took one small step   another

Rave Babies

from strollers   they luminesce
uplighting parent faces

with the same possibility
as uncracked glowsticks

drop rusks as they're
dropped off at nursery

by those who used to drop
discos   mix beats   but mostly

mix formula these days   4am
bottles checked against elbows

not 4am bass-woofers juddering
a cluster in strobing alcoves

those tenders of tiny diva riders
grabbing at hair   chubby

hands in the air   their *womp-
waaaaaah* dubby gurgles   pure

chemical potential   two elements
two genomes   twisted into a

fever dream   Sunday breakfast
wine   a daringly mingled line

they are raised from cots by arms
which poured themselves doubly triply

trippily into laser-arc sunrises   butter-
fingering for keys   far beyond dawn

fuzzy-tongued   sleep-deprived
the heave of cells undivided

how they might never know
how this slow henge of elders

strode through strobes & smoke
gave each other tokes   of advice

were each other's babies
a nonlinear raver lineage

each of us   poisoned   with love

Buy-A-Bear

in the store you shiver
> bypass the penguin aisle

select bear from a shelf
> of dissolving polystyrene

is it a real polar bear? you ask
> the till-girl *what*

do you think? she scoffs as she scans
  the barcode stapled to its rump

$420,000.50 beeps up, you pay
> on credit card for bear, hefty as

> though it is full of bones

the trolley wheels whimper

> *

you strap bear into the booster seat
  swivel its head towards the window
but it snaps back forward those
> piss-hole eyes staring right

into your mouth as you singsong
  there you go little bear
> *all safe & sound little bear*
> > *we'll soon be there little bear*

you go to hug bear
  but falter, unsure unprepared
> to brave those glossy

shrink-wrapped claws

> *

you keep bear in the fridge
    of course, partitioned from
the sausages, each day greet it
        sunnily *little bear* fun fact

their skin is actually black their fur
        transparent like polythene, you know this
          because now you see patches where
  fibres of muscle or whatever it has

in there might be, each day as you
      slam the door & cannot know
whether that light
            stays on

St Francis Christens the Animals in Notre-Dame, on Fire

Come forward, Brothers, Sisters all, to this font,
this pool of Sister Water – who is very useful
and humble and precious and chaste – and chase
her we must, for there is not enough of her
to extinguish this roof. Sisters, Brothers: bring me
your pups and younglings, the luminous green
commas of newborn chameleons; the translucent
spheres of the wormy platypus. I Christen them
amongst indoor asteroids, Brothers; altared ash,
Sisters. Throw me your babies, your bulge-eyed
chicks, pink like roast ortolan. Fling your lungfish,
I will try to catch them. And, if water is already
their element, I will raise them up to Brother Wind
and bless them in air. Beware the failing beams,
Sister-Brothers: the nave's fall. This font contains
Amazon, Yangtze, every river dammed to never
delta into epiphany. Hand me your infant pangolins
and I will sprinkle their scales like morning cloudburst,
my arm a dwindling canopy. This is my Canticle: my can-
tickle-tickle under those crusty armpits of your bonobo
bambinos. (Oh no, not now, Sister-Sisters – not *that*,
thank you.) Brother-Sisters, of course the frilly larvae
of axolotl are kin: all are in this pool of time, evaporating.
Can you see me through the smoke, Brother-Sisters?
Can you pray with paws and wings to Sister Water:
though precious and chaste, she cannot save this roof.
For, if He so wills it, this roof may resurrect again;
now pray to Father Capital, with all your claws and fins.

A Pink Sink

after Georgia Robinson's cover artwork

on our back garden wall   brimming like a punchbowl
its rogue eyeballs   raspberry globules   fruity polyps
a syrupy rainwater reduction a *gastropoda* aperitif
low self-seeded fascinator   its plinth a neck slurps
like gum from a rubber sole   and below
ground   a mucky mirror   viscous like vintage soup
in this slow-churn reflection   ants making their
underground deals   the tuber-nodes and grub-lumps
heaving up bodily   this sink   like the ones at after
after parties where sometimes I'd see at bowls
at basins   a perimeter of lime-green friendly
bacteria   swaying their flagella   in 4/4   a wave
of invitation   to flush myself   to dive into
the greening water table in full-throated harmony
with the pitcher plant mouths   of the subterranean

with the pitcher plant mouths of the subterranean
this greening water table in full-throated harmony
of invitation   to flush ourselves   to dive into
bacteria   swelling our flagella   in 4/4   a wave
at basins   a perimeter of lime-green friendly
after parties where sometimes we'd see   at bowls
heaving up bodily   this sink   like the ones after
underground deals   we tuber-nodes and grub-lumps
in this slow-churn reflection   ants making our
ground   a mucky mirror   viscous like vintage soup
stretching like gum from a rubber sole   and below
low self-seeded fascination   this plinth   a neck   slurps
a syrupy rainwater reduction   a *gastropoda* aperitif
its rogue eyeballs   raspberry globules   fruity polyps
on our back garden wall   brimming   like a punchbowl

Notes

In 'Whiptail Manifesto', obligate parthenogenesis is a form of asexual reproduction.

'The Landscape of Fear': epigraph from *The Atlantic* article, 'Nothing to Fear Except Fear Itself – Also Wolves and Bears', by Ed Yong, February 23rd 2016.

'19 Gigabecquerels' is inspired by the story of a lost Caesium-137 isotope being transported across the Australian outback, in January 2023. It was reportedly found later that month.

Muriel Howorth (1886-1971) championed the potential of atomic energy from 1948-1962. She focused on engaging women in citizen science and, in 1950, staged a ballet to illustrate subatomic structure. Howorth formed the Atomic Gardening Society in 1960, 'to promote the cultivation of gamma-irradiated seeds by British gardeners'.

'Our South African National Parks' started as part of a Queering the Museum commission with University of Exeter and RAMM Exeter, in 2021. The tobacco cards book is from 1941 and was inherited from my late grandmother.

'Nature Is (Not) Healing' is inspired by the wealth of memes created during lockdowns, lampooning this eco-ableist phrase.

'Mickey Pandemic' responds to the 2022 story of a Disney hand sanitiser, recalled after it was discovered to contain traces of carcinogens benzene and methanol.

'The Orca BnB' fuses a real stay at a dreadful BnB, with numerous reports of orcas attacking yachts in 2023. One theory suggests these attacks were spurred by a pod matriarch, who was injured by a boat and then taught younger orcas, leading to a culture of yacht attacks.

'Queertopia (Working Title)' references the Netflix documentary series *Wild Wild Country* (2018).

'GOLD' contains a fragment of dialogue from the movie *Goldfinger* (1964, Dir. Guy Hamilton).

Paul Dirac (1902-1984) was a Nobel Prize-winning mathematician from Bristol. He was neurodivergent at a time which did not recognise or accommodate this. His 'Dirac Equation' and other contributions to physics, while beyond public comprehension, were immense.

'What does cancer smell like to an ant?' riffs off research carried out by Professor Patrizia d'Etorre at Sorbonne Paris Nord University, training ants to detect cancers using patients' urine.

'Burying the Sky' is a form invented by Claire Collison, in which anagrams drawn from place names become the 'sonic landscape' of the poem (in this case, 'Diclofenac' and 'Doongerwadi dhakma').

The title for 'Narcissus Aesthetics: *Reflecting Perfection*' was created in collaboration with Chat GPT-4.

In 'Ten Reflections on the Same Pond', the phrase 'slow violence' is from Rob Nixon's *Slow Violence and the Environmentalism of the Poor* (Harvard University Press, 2011).

Acknowledgements and Thanks

Thanks to the following journals, where versions of some of these poems first appeared: *Berlin Lit; Butcher's Dog; Dreich; Ecopoetikon; Finished Creatures; Fruit; Ink, Sweat and Tears; Magma (84); Northern Gravy; Plumwood Mountain; Queerlings; Strix; Under the Radar*. 'Hornet' appears in *Twenty-One Poems About Wonky Animals* (Candlestick Press, 2022); 'Ricinus in Spring' in *After Sylvia: Poems and Essays in Celebration of Sylvia Plath* (Nine Arches, 2022). '19 Gigabecquerels' was Highly Commended in the Ginkgo Ecopoetry Prize 2022; 'Burying the Sky' and 'Two Tablespoonfuls' were longlisted in the Keats-Shelley Prize 2022. The latter also appears in *The Coin* (Broken Sleep) alongside 'learning to spell 'leukaemia''. 'The Landscape of Fear' appeared in the Broken Sleep anthology, *Masculinities: an anthology of modern voices*. 'Self-Portrait as Diary' was shortlisted for the Live Canon Single Poem Competition 2023. 'The Orca BnB' appears in the international anthology, *TEN SEA AIR*. 'I Found It Beautiful' was a commission to commemorate the work of Bristol Ideas and features in their publication, *Our Project Was the City* (Bristol Ideas, 2024).

Massive thanks to Jane and Angela at Nine Arches, as ever, for your editorial insight on this book and your dynamism in taking creative risks.

For cordial co-critique: Christina Thatcher, Simon Maddrell, Samuel Tongue, Luke Palmer, Pey Oh and Tessa Foley. Special thanks to Tom Sastry and Danny Pandolfi for companionship, beer, takeaway and poetry – when we eventually get to it.

Huge appreciation for Georgia Robinson's spectacular cover collage, inspired by these poems. Thanks to Elizabeth Parker for the inspiration to write a cover artwork ekphrastic poem, *inspired by that collage*. (So pleasing!)

To Polly Atkin, Andre Bagoo, and Suzannah Evans for your generous endorsements for this collection.

Some of these poems started during my PhD studentship as part of RENEW Biodiversity – with huge appreciation to Professor John Wedgwood Clarke, Dr Regan Early, and all those with whom I've had inspiring, interdisciplinary conversations.

Thanks to the organisations I work with across the poetry ecosystem: Poetry School, Arvon, Poetry Society, Literature Works.

Some of these poems are inspired by family members who face or have faced struggles. Thank you for inspiring these poems – I hope they do justice to my love and admiration for you.

With love and writhings to the Pack and ever-replenishing thanks for your support.

This collection is dedicated to my friends (and my foes). Shout out to all those whose presences are unruly, intoxicating and delicious. I love you all (even my foes).